Thomas Hardy
Selected Poems

W. Strang, portrait of Thomas Hardy (1893)

Selected Poems

Thomas Hardy

Collector's Poetry Library

This edition first published in 2004 by
COLLECTOR'S POETRY LIBRARY
an imprint of CRW Publishing Limited
69 Gloucester Crescent, London NW1 7EG

ISBN 1 904919 37 5

2 4 6 8 10 9 7 5 3 1

Typeset in Perpetua by Bookcraft Ltd,
Stroud, Gloucestershire, UK

Printed and bound in China by Imago

Contents

Introduction 9

Hap 17
She at His Funeral 17
Her Dilemma 18
Revulsion 18
She, to Him (II) 19
Neutral Tones 20
Her Initials 20
Her Immortality 21
The Ivy-Wife 23
Friends Beyond 24
Thoughts of Phena 26
'I Look Into My Glass' 27
Drummer Hodge 28
A Wife in London 29
Shelley's Skylark 30
To Life 31
The Subalterns 32
To an Unborn Pauper Child 34
Her Reproach 35
A Broken Appointment 36
His Immortality 37
The Darkling Thrush 38
The Self-Unseeing 39
In Tenebris (I) 40
In Tenebris (II) 41
In Tenebris (III) 42
Shut Out That Moon 45
1967 46
'I Say I'll Seek Her' 46
Her Confession 47

At Casterbridge Fair 48

The Minute Before Meeting 50

The Roman Road 50

The Man He Killed 51

Channel Firing 52

The Difference 53

'My Spirit Will Not Haunt the Mound' 54

Wessex Heights 54

Under the Waterfall 58

The Going 60

The Haunter 61

The Moon Looks In 63

Your Last Drive 64

The Voice 65

Exeunt Omnes 66

Moments of Vision 67

'We Sat at the Window' 68

Afternoon Service at Mellstock 68

At the Wicket-Gate 69

The Rival 70

Heredity 70

Before Knowledge 71

'The Wind Blew Words' 72

The Oxen 72

Transformations 73

The Last Signal 75

The Last Performance 76

Logs on the Hearth 76

In Time of 'The Breaking of Nations' 77

The Coming of the End 78

The Garden Seat 79

Afterwards 80

'I Sometimes Think' 81

'The Curtains Now Are Drawn' 82

Welcome Home 84
'A Man Was Drawing Near to Me' 84
The Strange House 87
A Night in November 88
The Selfsame Song 89
'She Did Not Turn' 89
A Two-Years' Idyll 90
'If You Had Known' 91
Epitaph 91
A Woman's Trust 92
Last Week in October 93
Ten Years Since 93
When Dead 94
Night-Time in Mid-Fall 94
Nobody Comes 95
No Buyers 96
'Nothing Matters Much' 97
'Why Do I?' 98
Thoughts at Midnight 99
The Love-Letters 100
The Mound 101
Evening Shadows 101
Throwing a Tree 102
The Lodging-House Fuchsias 103
Lying Awake 105
Suspense 105
Christmas: 1924 106
'We Are Getting to the End' 106
He Resolves to Say No More 107

Index of First Lines 109

Emma Lavinia Gifford

Introduction

THOMAS HARDY was born on 2 June 1840, at Higher Bockhampton, near Dorchester, England. He was educated at the village school, and at the age of 16 was apprenticed to the architect John Hicks. In his early twenties, his work took him to London, and it was there that he began writing, in his scarce spare time. By the age of 27 he had completed his first novel, *The Poor Man and the Lady*, but, dissatisfied with it, he destroyed the manuscript. By now working as Hicks's assistant, Hardy was sent to Cornwall in 1870, where he met his future wife, Emma Gifford.

Over the period of their courtship, Hardy published his first works: *Desperate Remedies* (1871), *Under the Greenwood Tree* (1872), and *A Pair of Blue Eyes* (1873). He and Emma were married in 1874: the year in which *Far From the Madding Crowd* was published, and the year in which Hardy made his reputation as a major novelist.

Over the next two decades, Hardy produced his most famous and successful works: *The Return of the Native* (1878), *The Mayor of Casterbridge* (1886), *Tess of the D'Urbervilles* (1891), and *Jude the Obscure* (1895). However, public and critical reaction to the perceived immorality of this last work led Hardy to declare in his diary 'the end of prose', and to abandon the art of the novel. For the last three decades of his life he dedicated himself to verse, writing over 900 poems. He received the Order of Merit in 1910. In 1912 Emma, from whom he had become estranged, died. He married his secretary, Florence Dugdale, in 1914, and collaborated with her on his autobiography, which was published posthumously (and under her name) in 1928, the year of his death.

It is perhaps surprising to learn that Thomas Hardy did not publish a volume of verse until he was nearly 60 and his first career, as a novelist, was over. He may be the only example of a major writer of English literature who has switched completely from one form to another, and been equally successful and prolific in both. This achievement is even more admirable when one considers that most of his poetry was new when it was published. Apart from *Wessex Poems* (1898, his first collection) and some of *Late Lyrics and Earlier* (1922), Hardy's poetical output did not rely on a large back catalogue. It represented new directions and new emphases for his writing, and dealt with a new world: Hardy's novels may be Victorian, but his poems are firmly rooted in the twentieth century.

For readers who come to this collection via Hardy the novelist, Hardy the poet will occupy both familiar and foreign territory. For the most part, particularly in the earlier poems (a slightly ridiculous phrase to use, considering the author was in his sixties), we are still in the Wessex which we know from *The Mayor of Casterbridge* or *The Woodlanders* (1887). The fictionalised towns of Budmouth, Mellstock or Christminster are occupied, in the poetry, by 'Friends Beyond' such as William Dewy and Tranter Reuben, whom we may recognise from some of the prose. We may also recognise Hardy's use of slightly antique, not-quite-dialect language. Furthermore, his love of nature, and his desire to relate wildlife and landscape to human emotion, is as strongly apparent in his verse as it is in his fiction, if not more so: 'Shelley's Skylark', 'The Darkling Thrush' and others from *Poems of the Past and the Present* (1901) are fine examples of this. Many of Hardy's novelistic themes are apparent as well: meditations on coincidence, on Fate, on the ravages of Time, and on the encroachment of the past onto the present (and occasionally, as in '1967' or 'The Strange House', the encroachment of the past onto the future), which may be familiar from works such as *The Mayor of Casterbridge*, are extended and developed here. However, the poems are by no means just a thematic reflection of Hardy's prose: in many ways, they are an attempt to focus on and crystallise those concerns which drove his earlier work.

As Hardy continues his poetic career, new and unfamiliar concerns begin to surface as well. Not surprisingly given that he was already in his sixties and seventies, anxieties over posterity, and what is left behind after death, begin to permeate his writing. And the twin weights of regret and bereavement hang heavy through his poetry collections, in a way that they do not in his novels.

Nowhere are these new themes more painfully apparent than in the material he wrote after Emma's death in 1912. Hardy's first marriage, which had been shaky for some considerable time, finally broke down in 1895 (the year in which *Jude* was published); and for their last decade-and-a-half he and Emma lived separately, but under one roof, exchanging barely a word with one another. Her death, however, released a tidal wave of unexpected and terrible grief, and of aching remorse, in the widower she left behind. From this point on, Hardy began writing what he called poems of 'expiation': the yearning, bitterly unhappy, yet extremely beautiful verses which first came to light in *Satires of Circumstance, Lyrics and Reveries* (1914). For many, these poems, which include 'The Going', 'The Voice' and 'Your Last Drive', are Hardy's finest and most touching works.

The poems from this point on become dominated by feelings of remorse, of bitterness, and of essential nothingness: 'No Buyers', 'Nobody Comes' and 'Nothing Matters Much' are all typical titles from his penultimate collection *Human Shows, Far Phantasies, Songs and Trifles* (1925). Just as Philip Larkin — a great admirer of Hardy — in his later poems seemed to see only death in all around him, so Hardy sees only pointlessness and futility. The calm matter-of-fact tone in which he dismisses human achievement in poems such as 'The Lodging House Fuchsias' or 'Christmas: 1924' ('After two thousand years of mass | We've got as far as poison gas'), both from his final collection, suggests a deep-rooted pessimism which, if anything, has come more sharply into focus over the years. The last poem in *Winter Words in Various Moods and Metres* (1928) is 'He Resolves to Say No More': a bitter parting-shot from a man who said so much over his long life, which recalls the unhappy decision concerning 'the end of prose' from 32 years earlier.

Peter Harness

Thomas and Florence Hardy

The forsaking of the Nest.

"The hoers quit the mangel-field.
 The firelight flecks the loam.
It is the minute of the hour
 She named to start for home.

"I see her step forth from the town
 And leave the lamps behind,
And trot along the eastern road
 Where elms stand double-lined.

"And now she nears the branching path,
 And takes the quicker way
Across the meadows where the brooks
 Glide gurgling night and day.

"By now she clacks the kissing-gate
 Beneath the storm-tried trees,
And passes to the second mead
 That fringes Mellstock Leaze.

"And soon she swings the wicket next
 The grey brick garden wall,
And sees the third mead stretching down
 Towards the waterfall.

T. O.

Manuscript of a poem published in 1912

Thomas Hardy

Selected Poems

My opinion is that a poet should express the emotion of all the ages and the thought of his own.

Thomas Hardy

HAP

IF but some vengeful god would call to me
From up the sky, and laugh: 'Thou suffering thing,
Know that thy sorrow is my ecstasy,
That thy love's loss is my hate's profiting!'

Then would I bear it, clench myself, and die,
Steeled by the sense of ire unmerited;
Half-eased in that a Powerfuller than I
Had willed and meted me the tears I shed.

But not so. How arrives it joy lies slain,
And why unblooms the best hope ever sown?
– Crass Casualty obstructs the sun and rain,
And dicing Time for gladness casts a moan. ...
These purblind Doomsters had as readily strown
Blisses about my pilgrimage as pain.

SHE AT HIS FUNERAL

THEY bear him to his resting-place –
In slow procession sweeping by;
I follow at a stranger's space;
His kindred they, his sweetheart I.
Unchanged my gown of garish dye,
Though sable-sad is their attire;
But they stand round with griefless eye,
Whilst my regret consumes like fire!

HER DILEMMA

(IN — CHURCH)

THE two were silent in a sunless church,
  Whose mildewed walls, uneven paving-stones,
And wasted carvings passed antique research;
And nothing broke the clock's dull monotones.

Leaning against a wormy poppy-head,
So wan and worn that he could scarcely stand,
— For he was soon to die, — he softly said,
'Tell me you love me!' — holding long her hand.

She would have given a world to breathe 'yes' truly,
So much his life seemed hanging on her mind,
And hence she lied, her heart persuaded throughly
'Twas worth her soul to be a moment kind.

But the sad need thereof, his nearing death,
So mocked humanity that she shamed to prize
A world conditioned thus, or care for breath
Where Nature such dilemmas could devise.

REVULSION

THOUGH I waste watches framing words to fetter
  Some unknown spirit to mine in clasp and kiss,
Out of the night there looms a sense 'twere better
To fail obtaining whom one fails to miss.

For winning love we win the risk of losing,
And losing love is as one's life were riven;
It cuts like contumely and keen ill-using
To cede what was superfluously given.

Let me then never feel the fateful thrilling
That devastates the love-worn wooer's frame,
The hot ado of fevered hopes, the chilling
That agonizes disappointed aim!
So may I live no junctive law fulfilling,
And my heart's table bear no woman's name.

SHE, TO HIM (II)

PERHAPS, long hence, when I have passed away,
   Some other's feature, accent, thought like mine,
Will carry you back to what I used to say,
And bring some memory of your love's decline.

Then you may pause awhile and think, 'Poor jade!'
And yield a sigh to me — as ample due,
Not as the tittle of a debt unpaid
To one who could resign her all to you —

And thus reflecting, you will never see
That your thin thought, in two small words conveyed,
Was no such fleeting phantom-thought to me,
But the Whole Life wherein my part was played;
And you amid its fitful masquerade
A Thought — as I in your life seem to be!

NEUTRAL TONES

WE stood by a pond that winter day,
    And the sun was white, as though chidden of God,
And a few leaves lay on the starving sod;
    — They had fallen from an ash, and were gray.

Your eyes on me were as eyes that rove
Over tedious riddles of years ago;
And some words played between us to and fro
    On which lost the more by our love.

The smile on your mouth was the deadest thing
Alive enough to have strength to die;
And a grin of bitterness swept thereby
    Like an ominous bird a-wing. ...

Since then, keen lessons that love deceives,
And wrings with wrong, have shaped to me
Your face, and the God-curst sun, and a tree,
    And a pond edged with grayish leaves.

HER INITIALS

UPON a poet's page I wrote
    Of old two letters of her name;
Part seemed she of the effulgent thought
Whence that high singer's rapture came.
    — When now I turn the leaf the same
Immortal light illumes the lay,
But from the letters of her name
The radiance has waned away!

HER IMMORTALITY

UPON a noon I pilgrimed through
A pasture, mile by mile,
Unto the place where last I saw
My dead Love's living smile.

And sorrowing I lay me down
Upon the heated sod:
It seemed as if my body pressed
The very ground she trod.

I lay, and thought; and in a trance
She came and stood thereby –
The same, even to the marvellous ray
That used to light her eye.

'You draw me, and I come to you,
My faithful one,' she said,
In voice that had the moving tone
It bore ere she was wed.

'Seven years have circled since I died:
Few now remember me;
My husband clasps another bride.
My children's love has she.

'My brethren, sisters, and my friends
Care not to meet my sprite:
Who prized me most I did not know
Till I passed down from sight.'

I said: 'My days are lonely here;
    I need thy smile alway:
I'll use this night my ball or blade,
    And join thee ere the day.'

A tremor stirred her tender lips,
    Which parted to dissuade:
'That cannot be, O friend,' she cried
    'Think, I am but a Shade!

'A Shade but in its mindful ones
    Has immortality;
By living, me you keep alive,
    By dying you slay me.

'In you resides my single power
    Of sweet continuance here;
On your fidelity I count
    Through many a coming year.'

– I started through me at her plight,
    So suddenly confessed:
Dismissing late distaste for life,
    I craved its bleak unrest.

'I will not die, my One of all! –
    To lengthen out thy days
I'll guard me from minutest harms
    That may invest my ways!'

She smiled and went. Since then she comes
    Oft when her birth-moon climbs,
Or at the seasons' ingresses,
    Or anniversary times;

But grows my grief. When I surcease,
　　Through whom alone lives she,
Her spirit ends its living lease,
　　Never again to be!

THE IVY-WIFE

I LONGED to love a full-boughed beech
　　And be as high as he:
I stretched an arm within his reach,
　　And signalled unity.
But with his drip he forced a breach,
　　And tried to poison me.

I gave the grasp of partnership
　　To one of other race —
A plane: he barked him strip by strip
　　From upper bough to base;
And me therewith; for gone my grip,
　　My arms could not enlace.

In new affection next I strove
　　To coll an ash I saw,
And he in trust received my love;
　　Till with my soft green claw
I cramped and bound him as I wove ...
　　Such was my love: ha-ha!

By this I gained his strength and height
　　Without his rivalry.
But in my triumph I lost sight
　　Of afterhaps. Soon he,
Being bark-bound, flagged, snapped, fell outright,
　　And in his fall felled me!

Friends Beyond

WILLIAM Dewy, Tranter Reuben,
          Farmer Ledlow late at plough,
   Robert's kin, and John's, and Ned's,
And the Squire, and Lady Susan,
         lie in Mellstock churchyard now!

'Gone,' I call them, gone for good,
         that group of local hearts and heads;
   Yet at mothy curfew-tide,
And at midnight when the noon-heat
         breathes it back from walls and leads,

They've a way of whispering to me –
         fellow-wight who yet abide –
   In the muted, measured note
Of a ripple under archways, or a lone cave's stillicide:

'We have triumphed: this achievement
         turns the bane to antidote,
   Unsuccesses to success,
Many thought-worn eves and morrows
         to a morrow free of thought.

'No more need we corn and clothing,
         feel of old terrestial stress:
   Chill detraction stirs no sigh;
Fear of death has even bygone us:
         death gave all that we possess.'

W. D.: 'Ye mid burn the old bass-viol
                              that I set such value by.'
Squire: 'You may hold the manse in fee,
You may wed my spouse, may let my children's
                              memory of me die.'

Lady S.: 'You may have my rich brocades, my laces;
                              take each household key;
     Ransack coffer, desk, bureau;
Quiz the few poor treasures hid there,
                              con the letters kept by me.'

Far.: 'Ye mid zell my favourite heifer,
                              ye mid let the charlock grow,
     Foul the grinterns, give up thrift.'
Far. Wife: 'If ye break my best blue china, children,
                              I shan't care or ho.'

All: 'We've no wish to hear the tidings,
                              how the people's fortunes shift;
     What your daily doings are;
Who are wedded, born, divided;
                              if your lives beat slow or swift.

'Curious not the least are we
                              if our intents you make or mar,
     If you quire to our old tune,
If the City stage still passes, if the weirs still roar afar.'

– Thus, with very gods' composure,
                              freed those crosses late and soon
     Which, in life, the Trine allow
(Why, none witteth), and ignoring all
                              that haps beneath the moon,

William Dewy, Tranter Reuben,
                        Farmer Ledlow late at plough,
  Robert's kin, and John's, and Ned's,
And the Squire, and Lady Susan,
                         murmur mildly to me now.

THOUGHTS OF PHENA

AT NEWS OF HER DEATH

NOT a line of her writing have I,
  Not a thread of her hair,
No mark of her late time
                as dame in her dwelling, whereby
  I may picture her there;
And in vain do I urge my unsight
  To conceive my lost prize
At her close, whom I knew
          when her dreams were upbrimming with light,
  And with laughter her eyes.

What scenes spread around her last days,
  Sad, shining, or dim?
Did her gifts and compassions
                enray and enarch her sweet ways
  With an aureate nimb?
Or did life-light decline from her years,
  And mischances control
Her full day-star; unease, or regret,
              or forebodings, or fears
  Disennoble her soul?

Thus I do but the phantom retain
   Of the maiden of yore
As my relic; yet haply the best of her – fined in my brain
   It may be the more
That no line of her writing have I,
   Nor a thread of her hair,
No mark of her late time
                   as dame in her dwelling, whereby
   I may picture her there.

'I LOOK INTO MY GLASS'

I LOOK into my glass,
  And view my wasting skin,
And say, 'Would God it came to pass
  My heart had shrunk as thin!'

For then, I, undistrest
  By hearts grown cold to me,
Could lonely wait my endless rest
  With equanimity.

But Time, to make me grieve,
  Part steals, lets part abide;
And shakes this fragile frame at eve
  With throbbings of noontide.

DRUMMER HODGE

I

THEY throw in Drummer Hodge, to rest
    Uncoffined just as found:
His landmark is a kopje-crest
    That breaks the veldt around;
And foreign constellations west
    Each night above his mound.

II

Young Hodge the Drummer never knew —
    Fresh from his Wessex home —
The meaning of the broad Karoo,
    The Bush, the dusty loam,
And why uprose to nightly view
    Strange stars amid the gloam.

III

Yet portion of that unknown plain
    Will Hodge for ever be;
His homely Northern breast and brain
    Grow to some Southern tree,
And strange-eyed constellations reign
    His stars eternally.

A WIFE IN LONDON

December 1899

I

SHE sits in the tawny vapour
That the Thames-side lanes have uprolled,
  Behind whose webby fold on fold
Like a waning taper
  The street-lamp glimmers cold.

A messenger's knock cracks smartly,
  Flashed news is in her hand
  Of meaning it dazes to understand
Though shaped so shortly:
  He — has fallen — in the far South Land. ...

II

'Tis the morrow; the fog hangs thicker,
  The postman nears and goes:
  A letter is brought whose lines disclose
By the firelight flicker
  His hand, whom the worm now knows:

Fresh — firm — penned in highest feather —
  Page-full of his hoped return,
  And of home-planned jaunts by brake and burn
In the summer weather,
  And of new love that they would learn.

SHELLEY'S SKYLARK

The neighbourhood of Leghorn: March 1887

SOMEWHERE afield here something lies
In Earth's oblivious eyeless trust
That moved a poet to prophecies –
A pinch of unseen, unguarded dust:

The dust of the lark that Shelley heard,
And made immortal through times to be; –
Though it only lived like another bird,
And knew not its immortality:

Lived its meek life; then, one day, fell –
A little ball of feather and bone;
And how it perished, when piped farewell,
And where it wastes, are alike unknown.

Maybe it rests in the loam I view,
Maybe it throbs in a myrtle's green,
Maybe it sleeps in the coming hue
Of a grape on the slopes of yon inland scene.

Go find it, faeries, go and find
That tiny pinch of priceless dust,
And bring a casket silver-lined,
And framed of gold that gems encrust;

And we will lay it safe therein,
And consecrate it to endless time;
For it inspired a bard to win
Ecstatic heights in thought and rhyme.

To Life

O LIFE with the sad seared face,
   I weary of seeing thee,
And thy draggled cloak, and thy hobbling pace,
   And thy too-forced pleasantry!

I know what thou would'st tell
   Of Death, Time, Destiny —
I have known it long, and know, too, well
   What it all means for me.

But canst thou not array
   Thyself in rare disguise,
And feign like truth, for one mad day,
   That Earth is Paradise?

I'll tune me to the mood,
   And mumm with thee till eve;
And maybe what as interlude
   I feign, I shall believe!

THE SUBALTERNS

I

' POOR wanderer,' said the leaden sky,
    'I fain would lighten thee,
But there are laws in force on high
    Which say it must not be.'

II

— 'I would not freeze thee, shorn one,' cried
    The North, 'knew I but how
To warm my breath, to slack my stride;
    But I am ruled as thou.'

III

— 'Tomorrow I attack thee, wight,'
    Said Sickness. 'Yet I swear
I bear thy little ark no spite,
    But am bid enter there.'

IV

— 'Come hither, Son,' I heard Death say;
    'I did not will a grave
Should end thy pilgrimage today,
    But I, too, am a slave!'

V

We smiled upon each other then,
    And life to me had less
Of that fell look it wore ere when
    They owned their passiveness.

Constant Troyon, 'The Approaching Storm' (1849)

TO AN UNBORN PAUPER CHILD

I

BREATHE not, hid Heart: cease silently,
　And though thy birth-hour beckons thee,
　　Sleep the long sleep:
　　The Doomsters heap
　Travails and teens around us here,
And Time-wraiths turn our songsingings to fear.

II

　Hark, how the peoples surge and sigh,
　And laughters fail, and greetings die:
　　Hopes dwindle; yea,
　　Faiths waste away,
　Affections and enthusiasms numb;
Thou canst not mend these things if thou dost come.

III

　Had I the ear of wombèd souls
　Ere their terrestrial chart unrolls,
　　And thou wert free
　　To cease, or be,
　Then would I tell thee all I know,
And put it to thee: Wilt thou take Life so?

IV

Vain vow! No hint of mine may hence
To theeward fly: to thy locked sense
    Explain none can
    Life's pending plan:
Thou wilt thy ignorant entry make
Though skies spout fire and blood and nations quake.

V

Fain would I, dear, find some shut plot
Of earth's wide wold for thee, where not
    One tear, one qualm,
    Should break the calm.
But I am weak as thou and bare;
No man can change the common lot to rare.

VI

Must come and bide. And such are we —
Unreasoning, sanguine, visionary —
    That I can hope
    Health, love, friends, scope
In full for thee; can dream thou'lt find
Joys seldom yet attained by humankind!

HER REPROACH

CON the dead page as 'twere live love: press on!
  Cold wisdom's words will ease thy track for thee;
Aye, go; cast off sweet ways, and leave me wan
To biting blasts that are intent on me.

But if thy object Fame's far summits be,
Whose inclines many a skeleton overlies
That missed both dream and substance, stop and see
How absence wears these cheeks and dims these eyes!

It surely is far sweeter and more wise
To water love, than toil to leave anon
A name whose glory-gleam will but advise
Invidious minds to eclipse it with their own,

And over which the kindliest will but stay
A moment; musing, 'He, too, had his day!'

A Broken Appointment

You did not come,
And marching Time drew on,
and wore me numb. —
Yet less for loss of your dear presence there
Than that I thus found lacking in your make
That high compassion which can overbear
Reluctance for pure lovingkindness' sake
Grieved I, when, as the hope-hour stroked its sum,
You did not come.

You love not me,
And love alone can lend you loyalty;
— I know and knew it. But, unto the store
Of human deeds divine in all but name,
Was it not worth a little hour or more
To add yet this: Once you, á woman, came
To soothe a time-torn man; even though it be
You love not me?

HIS IMMORTALITY

I

I SAW a dead man's finer part
  Shining within each faithful heart
Of those bereft. Then said I: 'This must be
  His immortality.'

II

I looked there as the seasons wore,
And still his soul continuously bore
A life in theirs. But less its shine excelled
  Than when I first beheld.

III

His fellow-yearsmen passed, and then
In later hearts I looked for him again;
And found him – shrunk, alas! into a thin
  And spectral mannikin.

IV

Lastly I ask – now old and chill –
If aught of him remain unperished still;
And find, in me alone, a feeble spark,
  Dying amid the dark.

THE DARKLING THRUSH

I LEANT upon a coppice gate
        When Frost was spectre-gray,
And Winter's dregs made desolate
        The weakening eye of day.
The tangled bine-stems scored the sky
        Like strings of broken lyres,
And all mankind that haunted nigh
        Had sought their household fires.

The land's sharp features seemed to be
        The Century's corpse outleant,
His crypt the cloudy canopy,
        The wind his death-lament.
The ancient pulse of germ and birth
        Was shrunken hard and dry,
And every spirit upon earth
        Seemed fervourless as I.

At once a voice arose among
        The bleak twigs overhead
In a full-hearted evensong
        Of joy illimited;
An aged thrush, frail, gaunt, and small,
        In blast-beruffled plume,
Had chosen thus to fling his soul
        Upon the growing gloom.

So little cause for carolings
    Of such ecstatic sound
Was written on terrestrial things
    Afar or nigh around,
That I could think there trembled through
    His happy good-night air
Some blessed Hope, whereof he knew
    And I was unaware.

THE SELF-UNSEEING

HERE is the ancient floor,
Footworn and hollowed and thin,
Here was the former door
Where the dead feet walked in.

She sat here in her chair,
Smiling into the fire;
He who played stood there,
Bowing it higher and higher.

Childlike, I danced in a dream;
Blessings emblazoned that day;
Everything glowed with a gleam;
Yet we were looking away!

In Tenebris (I)

Percussus sum sicut foenum, et aruit cor meum. —— Psalm ci

WINTERTIME nighs;
　　But my bereavement-pain
It cannot bring again:
　　Twice no one dies.

Flower-petals flee;
But, since it once hath been,
No more that severing scene
　　Can harrow me.

Birds faint in dread:
I shall not lose old strength
In the lone frost's black length:
　　Strength long since fled!

Leaves freeze to dun;
But friends can not turn cold
This season as of old
　　For him with none.

Tempests may scath;
But love can not make smart
Again this year his heart
　　Who no heart bath.

Black is night's cope;
But death will not appal
One who, past doubtings all,
　　Waits in unhope.

IN TENEBRIS (II)

*Considerabam ad dexteram, et videbam; et non erat qui cognosceret
me. ... Non est qui requirat animam meam.* — Psalm cxli

WHEN the clouds' swoln bosoms echo back
          the shouts of the many and strong
That things are all as they best may be,
          save a few to be right ere long,
And my eyes have not the vision in them
          to discern what to these is so clear,
The blot seems straightway in me alone;
          one better he were not here.

The stout upstanders say,
          All's well with us: ruers have nought to rue!
And what the potent say so oft,
          can it fail to be somewhat true?
Breezily go they, breezily come;
          their dust smokes around their career,
Till I think l am one born out of due time,
          who has no calling here.

Their dawns bring lusty joys, it seems;
          their evenings all that is sweet;
Our times are blessed times, they cry:
          Life shapes it as is most meet,
And nothing is much the matter;
          there are many smiles to a tear;
Then what is the matter is I, I say.
          Why should such an one be here? ...

Let him in whose ears the low-voiced Best
　　　　　　is killed by the clash of the First,
Who holds that if way to the Better there be,
　　　　　　it exacts a full look at the Worst,
Who feels that delight is a delicate growth
　　　　　　cramped by crookedness, custom, and fear,
Get him up and be gone as one shaped awry;
　　　　　　he disturbs the order here.

In Tenebris (III)

*Heu mihi, quia incolatus meus prolongatus est! Habitavi cum
habitantibus Cedar; multum incola fuit anima mea.* — Psalm cxix

THERE have been times when I well might have passed
　　　　　　and the ending have come –
Points in my path when the dark
　　　　　　might have stolen on me, artless, unrueing –
Ere I had learnt that the world
　　　　　　was a welter of futile doing:
Such had been times when I well might have passed,
　　　　　　and the ending have come!

Say, on the noon when the half-sunny hours
　　　　　　told that April was nigh,
And I upgathered and cast forth the snow
　　　　　　from the crocus-border,
Fashioned and furbished the soil
　　　　　　into a summer-seeming order,
Glowing in gladsome faith
　　　　　　that I quickened the year thereby.

Or on that loneliest of eves
              when afar and benighted we stood,
She who upheld me and I,
              in the midmost of Egdon together,
Confident I in her watching and ward
              through the blackening heather,
Deeming her matchless in might
              and with measureless scope endued.

Or on that winter-wild night when,
              reclined by the chimney-nook quoin,
Slowly a drowse overgat me,
              the smallest and feeblest of folk there,
Weak from my baptism of pain;
              when at times and anon I awoke there –
Heard of a world wheeling on,
              with no listing or longing to join.

Even then! while unweeting that vision could vex
              or that knowledge could numb,
That sweets to the mouth in the belly
              are bitter, and tart, and untoward,
Then, on some dim-coloured scene
              should my briefly raised curtain have lowered,
Then might the Voice that is law have said 'Cease!'
              and the ending have come.

Jean-Baptiste-Siméon Chardin, 'The Silver Cup'

SHUT OUT THAT MOON

CLOSE up the casement, draw the blind,
　　Shut out that stealing moon,
She wears too much the guise she wore
　　Before our lutes were strewn
With years-deep dust, and names we read
　　On a white stone were hewn.

Step not forth on the dew-dashed lawn
　　To view the Lady's Chair.
Immense Orion's glittering form,
　　The Less and Greater Bear:
Stay in; to such sights we were drawn
　　When faded ones were fair.

Brush not the bough for midnight scents
　　That come forth lingeringly,
And wake the same sweet sentiments
　　They breathed to you and me
When living seemed a laugh, and love
　　All it was said to be.

Within the common lamp-lit room
　　Prison my eyes and thought;
Let dingy details crudely loom,
　　Mechanic speech be wrought:
Too fragrant was Life's early bloom,
　　Too tart the fruit it brought!

1967

IN five-score summers! All new eyes,
New minds, new modes, new fools, new wise;
New woes to weep, new joys to prize;

With nothing left of me and you
In that live century's vivid view
Beyond a pinch of dust or two;

A century which, if not sublime,
Will show, I doubt not, at its prime,
A scope above this blinkered time.

— Yet what to me how far above?
For I would only ask thereof
That thy worm should be my worm, Love!

'I Say I'll Seek Her'

I SAY, 'I'll seek her side
Ere hindrance interposes;'
    But eve in midnight closes,
And here I still abide.

When darkness wears I see
    Her sad eyes in a vision;
    They ask, 'What indecision
Detains you, Love, from me? —

'The creaking hinge is oiled,
    I have unbarred the backway,
    But you tread not the trackway
And shall the thing be spoiled?

'Far cockcrows echo shrill,
  The shadows are abating,
  And I am waiting, waiting;
But O, you tarry still!'

HER CONFESSION

As some bland soul, to whom a debtor says
'I'll now repay the amount I owe to you,'
In inward gladness feigns forgetfulness
That such a payment ever was his due

(His long thought notwithstanding), so did I
At our last meeting waive your proffered kiss
With quick divergent talk of scenery nigh,
By such suspension to enhance my bliss.

And as his looks in consternation fall
When, gathering that the debt is lightly deemed,
The debtor makes as not to pay at all,
So faltered I, when your intention seemed

Converted by my false uneagerness
To putting off for ever the caress.

AT CASTERBRIDGE FAIR

VII
AFTER THE FAIR

THE singers are gone from the Cornmarket-place
    With their broadsheets of rhymes,
The street rings no longer in treble and bass
    With their skits on the times,
And the Cross, lately thronged, is a dim naked space
    That but echoes the stammering chimes.

From Clock-corner steps, as each quarter ding-dongs,
    Away the folk roam
By the 'Hart' and Grey's Bridge
                        into byways and 'drongs,'
    Or across the ridged loam;
The younger ones shrilling the lately heard songs,
    The old saying, 'Would we were home.'

The shy-seeming maiden so mute in the fair
    Now rattles and talks,
And that one who looked the most swaggering there
    Grows sad as she walks,
And she who seemed eaten by cankering care
    In statuesque sturdiness stalks.

And midnight clears High Street of all but the ghosts
    Of its buried burghees,
From the latest far back to those old Roman hosts
    Whose remains one yet sees,
Who loved, laughed, and fought,
                        hailed their friends, drank their toasts
    At their meeting-times here, just as these!

High Place Hall, Casterbridge

THE MINUTE BEFORE MEETING

THE grey gaunt days dividing us in twain
    Seemed hopeless hills
                    my strength must faint to climb,
But they are gone; and now I would detain
The few clock-beats that part us; rein back Time,

And live in close expectance never closed
In change for far expectance closed at last,
So harshly has expectance been imposed
On my long need while these slow blank months passed.

And knowing that what is now about to be
Will all *have been* in O, so short a space!
I read beyond it my despondency
When more dividing months shall take its place,
Thereby denying to this hour of grace
A full-up measure of felicity.

THE ROMAN ROAD

THE Roman Road runs straight and bare
    As the pale parting-line in hair
Across the heath. And thoughtful men
Contrast its days of Now and Then,
And delve, and measure, and compare;

Visioning on the vacant air
Helmed legionaries, who proudly rear
The Eagle, as they pace again
    The Roman Road.

But no tall brass-helmed legionnaire
Haunts it for me. Uprises there
A mother's form upon my ken,
Guiding my infant steps, as when
We walked that ancient thoroughfare,
   The Roman Road.

THE MAN HE KILLED

' HAD he and I but met
    By some old ancient inn,
We should have sat us down to wet
   Right many a nipperkin!

'But ranged as infantry,
   And staring face to face,
I shot at him as he at me,
   And killed him in his place.

'I shot him dead because —
   Because he was my foe,
Just so: my foe of course he was:
   That's clear enough; although

'He thought he'd 'list, perhaps,
   Off-hand like — just as I —
Was out of work — had sold his traps —
   No other reason why.

'Yes; quaint and curious war is!
   You shoot a fellow down
You'd treat if met where any bar is,
   Or help to half-a-crown.'

CHANNEL FIRING

THAT night your great guns, unawares,
 Shook all our coffins as we lay,
And broke the chancel window-squares,
We thought it was the Judgment-day

And sat upright. While drearisome
Arose the howl of wakened hounds:
The mouse let fall the altar-crumb,
The worms drew back into the mounds,

The glebe cow drooled. Till God called, 'No;
It's gunnery practice out at sea
Just as before you went below;
The world is as it used to be:

'All nations striving strong to make
Red war yet redder. Mad as hatters
They do no more for Christés sake
Than you who are helpless in such matters.

'That this is not the judgment-hour
For some of them's a blessed thing,
For if it were they'd have to scour
Hell's floor for so much threatening. ...

'Ha, ha. It will be warmer when
I blow the trumpet (if indeed
I ever do; for you are men,
And rest eternal sorely need).'

So down we lay again. 'I wonder,
Will the world ever saner be,'
Said one, 'than when He sent us under
In our indifferent century!'

And many a skeleton shook his head.
'Instead of preaching forty year,'
My neighbour Parson Thirdly said,
'I wish I had stuck to pipes and beer.'

Again the guns disturbed the hour,
Roaring their readiness to avenge,
As far inland as Stourton Tower,
And Camelot, and starlit Stonehenge.

THE DIFFERENCE

I

SINKING down by the gate I discern the thin moon,
And a blackbird tries over old airs in the pine,
But the moon is a sorry one, sad the bird's tune,
For this spot is unknown to that Heartmate of mine.

II

Did my Heartmate but haunt here at times such as now,
The song would be joyous and cheerful the moon;
But she will see never this gate, path, or bough,
Nor I find a joy in the scene or the tune.

'MY SPIRIT WILL NOT HAUNT THE MOUND'

MY spirit will not haunt the mound
 Above my breast,
But travel, memory-possessed,
To where my tremulous being found
 Life largest, best.

My phantom-footed shape will go
 When nightfall grays
Hither and thither along the ways
I and another used to know
 In backward days.

And there you'll find me, if a jot
 You still should care
For me, and for my curious air;
If otherwise, then I shall not,
 For you, be there.

WESSEX HEIGHTS

1896

THERE are some heights in Wessex,
     shaped as if by a kindly hand
For thinking, dreaming, dying on,
      and at crises when I stand,
Say, on Ingpen Beacon eastward,
     or on Wylls-Neck westwardly,
I seem where I was before my birth,
     and after death may be.

In the lowlands I have no comrade,
          not even the lone man's friend —
Her who suffereth long and is kind;
          accepts what he is too weak to mend:
Down there they are dubious and askance;
          there nobody thinks as I,
But mind-chains do not clank
          where one's next neighbour is the sky.

In the towns I am tracked by phantoms
          having weird detective ways —
Shadows of beings who fellowed with
          myself of earlier days:
They hang about at places,
          and they say harsh heavy things —
Men with a wintry sneer,
          and women with tart disparagings.

Down there I seem to be false to myself,
          my simple self that was,
And is not now, and I see him watching,
          wondering what crass cause
Can have merged him into such a strange continuator
          as this,
Who yet has something in common with himself,
          my chrysalis.

I cannot go to the great grey Plain; there's a figure
                              against the moon,
Nobody sees it but I, and it makes my breast
                              beat out of tune;
I cannot go to the tall-spired town,
                    being barred by the forms now passed
For everybody but me, in whose long vision
                              they stand there fast.

There's a ghost at Yell'ham Bottom
                    chiding loud at the fall of the night,
There's a ghost in Froom-side Vale,
                    thin-lipped and vague, in a shroud of white,
There is one in the railway train
                    whenever I do not want it near,
I see its profile against the pane,
                    saying what I would not hear.

As for one rare fair woman,
                    I am now but a thought of hers,
I enter her mind and another thought succeeds me
                    that she prefers;
Yet my love for her in its fulness
                    she herself even did not know;
Well, time cures hearts of tenderness,
                    and now I can let her go.

So I am found on Ingpen Beacon,
                    or on Wylls-Neck to the west,
Or else on homely Bulbarrow, or little Pilsdon Crest,
Where men have never cared to haunt,
                    nor women have walked with me,
And ghosts then keep their distance;
                    and I know some liberty.

Hardy's own map of Wessex

UNDER THE WATERFALL

'WHENEVER I plunge my arm, like this,
    In a basin of water, I never miss
The sweet sharp sense of a fugitive day
Fetched back from its thickening shroud of gray.
    Hence the only prime
    And real love-rhyme
    That I know by heart,
    And that leaves no smart,
Is the purl of a little valley fall
About three spans wide and two spans tall
Over a table of solid rock,
And into a scoop of the self-same block;
The purl of a runlet that never ceases
In stir of kingdoms, in wars, in peaces;
With a hollow boiling voice it speaks
And has spoken since hills were turfless peaks.'

'And why gives this the only prime
Idea to you of a real love-rhyme?
And why does plunging your arm in a bowl
Full of spring water, bring throbs to your soul?'

'Well, under the fall, in a crease of the stone,
Though where precisely none ever has known,
Jammed darkly, nothing to show how prized,
And by now with its smoothness opalized,
   Is a drinking-glass:
   For, down that pass
   My lover and I
   Walked under a sky
Of blue with a leaf-wove awning of green,
In the burn of August, to paint the scene,
And we placed our basket of fruit and wine
By the runlet's rim, where we sat to dine;
And when we had drunk from the glass together,
Arched by the oak-copse from the weather,
I held the vessel to rinse in the fall,
Where it slipped, and sank, and was past recall,
Though we stooped and plumbed the little abyss
With long bared arms. There the glass still is.
And, as said, if I thrust my arm below
Cold water in basin or bowl, a throe
From the past awakens a sense of that time,
And the glass we used, and the cascade's rhyme.
The basin seems the pool, and its edge
The hard smooth face of the brook-side ledge,
And the leafy pattern of china-ware
The hanging plants that were bathing there.

'By night, by day, when it shines or lours,
There lies intact that chalice of ours,
And its presence adds to the rhyme of love
Persistently sung by the fall above.
No lip has touched it since his and mine
In turns therefrom sipped lovers' wine.'

THE GOING

WHY did you give no hint that night
  That quickly after the morrow's dawn,
And calmly, as if indifferent quite,
You would close your term here, up and be gone
    Where I could not follow.
    With wing of swallow
To gain one glimpse of you ever anon!

    Never to bid good-bye,
      Or lip me the softest call,
Or utter a wish for a word, while I
Saw morning harden upon the wall,
    Unmoved, unknowing
    That your great going
Had place that moment, and altered all.

Why do you make me leave the house
And think for a breath it is you I see
At the end of the alley of bending boughs
Where so often at dusk you used to be;
    Till in darkening dankness
    The yawning blankness
Of the perspective sickens me!

    You were she who abode
      By those red-veined rocks far West,
You were the swan-necked one who rode
Along the beetling Beeny Crest,
    And, reining nigh me,
    Would muse and eye me,
While Life unrolled us its very best.

Why, then, latterly did we not speak,
Did we not think of those days long dead,
And ere your vanishing strive to seek
That time's renewal? We might have said,
   'In this bright spring weather
   We'll visit together
Those places that once we visited.'

   Well, well! All's past amend,
   Unchangeable. It must go.
I seem but a dead man held on end
To sink down soon. ... O you could not know
   That such swift fleeing
   No soul foreseeing –
Not even I – would undo me so!

THE HAUNTER

HE does not think that I haunt here nightly:
   How shall I let him know
That whither his fancy sets him wandering
   I, too, alertly go? –
Hover and hover a few feet from him
   Just as I used to do,
But cannot answer the words he lifts me –
   Only listen thereto!

When I could answer he did not say them:
    When I could let him know
How I would like to join in his journeys
    Seldom he wished to go.
Now that he goes and wants me with him
    More than he used to do,
Never he sees my faithful phantom
    Though he speaks thereto.

Yes, I companion him to places
    Only dreamers know,
Where the shy hares print long paces,
    Where the night rooks go;
Into old aisles where the past is all to him,
    Close as his shade can do,
Always lacking the power to call to him,
    Near as I reach thereto!

What a good haunter I am, O tell him!
    Quickly make him know
If he but sigh since my loss befell him
    Straight to his side I go.
Tell him a faithful one is doing
    All that love can do
Still that his path may be worth pursuing,
    And to bring peace thereto.

THE MOON LOOKS IN

I

I HAVE risen again,
And awhile survey
By my chilly ray
Through your window pane
Your upturned face,
As you think, 'Ah – she
Now dreams of me
In her distant place!'

II

I pierce her blind
In her far-off home:
She fixes a comb,
And says in her mind,
'I start in an hour;
Whom shall I meet?
Won't the men be sweet,
And the women sour!'

YOUR LAST DRIVE

HERE by the moorway you returned,
  And saw the borough lights ahead
That lit your face – all undiscerned
To be in a week the face of the dead,
And you told of the charm of that haloed view
That never again would beam on you.

And on your left you passed the spot
Where eight years later you were to lie,
And be spoken of as one who was not;
Beholding it with a heedless eye
As alien from you, though under its tree
You soon would halt everlastingly.

I drove not with you. ... Yet had I sat
At your side that eve I should not have seen
That the countenance I was glancing at
Had a last-time look in the flickering sheen,
Nor have read the writing upon your face,
'I go hence soon to my resting-place;

'You may miss me then. But I shall not know
How many times you visit me there,
Or what your thoughts are, or if you go
There never at all. And I shall not care.
Should you censure me I shall take no heed,
And even your praises no more shall need.'

True: never you'll know. And you will not mind.
But shall I then slight you because of such?
Dear ghost, in the past did you ever find
The thought 'What profit,' move me much?
Yet abides the fact, indeed, the same, –
You are past love, praise, indifference, blame.

THE VOICE

Woman much missed,
                    how you call to me, call to me,
Saying that now you are not as you were
When you had changed from the one who was all to me,
But as at first, when our day was fair.

Can it be you that I hear? Let me view you, then,
Standing as when I drew near to the town
Where you would wait for me: yes, as I knew you then,
Even to the original air-blue gown!

Or is it only the breeze, in its listlessness
Travelling across the wet mead to me here,
You being ever dissolved to wan wistlessness,
Heard no more again far or near?

   Thus I; faltering forward,
   Leaves around me falling,
Wind oozing thin through the thorn from norward
   And the woman calling.

Exeunt Omnes

I

E VERYBODY else, then, going,
   And I still left where the fair was? ...
Much have I seen of neighbour loungers
   Making a lusty showing,
   Each now past all knowing.

II

   There is an air of blankness
In the street and the littered spaces;
Thoroughfare, steeple, bridge and highway
   Wizen themselves to lankness;
   Kennels dribble dankness.

III

   Folk all fade. And whither,
As I wait alone where the fair was?
Into the clammy and numbing night-fog
   Whence they entered hither.
   Soon one more goes thither!

MOMENTS OF VISION

THAT mirror
  Which makes of men a transparency,
   Who holds that mirror
And bids us such a breast-bare spectacle see
    Of you and me?

  That mirror
  Whose magic penetrates like a dart,
   Who lifts that mirror
And throws our mind back on us, and our heart,
    Until we start?

  That mirror
  Works well in these night hours of ache;
   Why in that mirror
Are tincts we never see ourselves once take
    When the world is awake?

  That mirror
  Can test each mortal when unaware;
   Yea, that strange mirror
May catch his last thoughts, whole life foul or fair,
    Glassing it – where?

'We Sat at the Window'

Bournemouth, 1875

W E sat at the window looking out,
        And the rain came down like silken strings
That Swithin's day. Each gutter and spout
Babbled unchecked in the busy way
        Of witless things:
Nothing to read, nothing to see
Seemed in that room for her and me
        On Swithin's day.

We were irked by the scene, by our own selves; yes.
For I did not know, nor did she infer
How much there was to read and guess
By her in me, and to see and crown
        By me in her.
Wasted were two souls in their prime,
And great was the waste, that July time
        When the rain came down.

Afternoon Service at Mellstock

Circa 1850

O N afternoons of drowsy calm
        We stood in the panelled pew,
Singing one-voiced a Tate-and-Brady psalm
        To the tune of 'Cambridge New.'

    We watched the elms, we watched the rooks,
        The clouds upon the breeze,
Between the whiles of glancing at our books,
        And swaying like the trees.

So mindless were those outpourings! —
   Though I am not aware
That I have gained by subtle thought on things
   Since we stood psalming there.

AT THE WICKET-GATE

THERE floated the sounds of church-chiming,
   But no one was nigh,
Till there came, as a break in the loneness,
   Her father, she, I.
And we slowly moved on to the wicket,
   And downlooking stood,
Till anon people passed, and amid them
   We parted for good.

Greater, wiser, may part there than we three
   Who parted there then,
But never will Fates colder-featured
   Hold sway there again.
Of the churchgoers through the still meadows
   No single one knew
What a play was played under their eyes there
   As thence we withdrew.

THE RIVAL

I DETERMINED to find out whose it was —
  The portrait he looked at so, and sighed;
Bitterly have I rued my meanness
    And wept for it since he died!

I searched his desk when he was away,
  And there was the likeness — yes, my own!
Taken when I was the season's fairest,
    And time-lines all unknown.

I smiled at my image, and put it back,
  And he went on cherishing it, until
I was chafed that he loved not the me then living,
    But that past woman still.

Well, such was my jealousy at last,
  I destroyed that face of the former me;
Could you ever have dreamed the heart of woman
    Would work so foolishly!

HEREDITY

I AM the family face;
  Flesh perishes, I live on,
Projecting trait and trace
Through time to times anon,
And leaping from place to place
Over oblivion.

The years-heired feature that can
In curve and voice and eye
Despise the human span
Of durance – that is I;
The eternal thing in man,
That heeds no call to die.

BEFORE KNOWLEDGE

WHEN I walked roseless tracks and wide,
  Ere dawned your date for meeting me,
O why did you not cry Halloo
Across the stretch between, and say:

'We move, while years as yet divide,
On closing lines which – though it be
You know me not nor I know you –
Will intersect and join some day!'

Then well I had borne
Each scraping thorn;
But the winters froze,
And grew no rose;
No bridge bestrode
The gap at all;
No shape you showed,
And I heard no call!

'THE WIND BLEW WORDS'

THE wind blew words along the skies,
    And these it blew to me
Through the wide dusk: 'Lift up your eyes,
    Behold this troubled tree,
Complaining as it sways and plies;
    It is a limb of thee.

'Yea, too, the creatures sheltering round —
    Dumb figures, wild and tame,
Yea, too, thy fellows who abound —
    Either of speech the same
Or far and strange — black, dwarfed, and browned,
    They are stuff of thy own frame.'

I moved on in a surging awe
    Of inarticulateness
At the pathetic Me I saw
    In all his huge distress,
Making self-slaughter of the law
    To kill, break, or suppress.

THE OXEN

CHRISTMAS Eve, and twelve of the clock.
    'Now they are all on their knees,'
An elder said as we sat in a flock
    By the embers in hearthside ease.

We pictured the meek mild creatures where
    They dwelt in their strawy pen,
Nor did it occur to one of us there
    To doubt they were kneeling then.

So fair a fancy few would weave
   In these years! Yet, I feel,
If someone said on Christmas Eve,
   'Come; see the oxen kneel

'In the lonely barton by yonder coomb
   Our childhood used to know,'
I should go with him in the gloom,
   Hoping it might be so.

Transformations

PORTION of this yew
   Is a man my grandsire knew,
Bosomed here at its foot:
This branch may be his wife,
A ruddy human life
Now turned to a green shoot.

These grasses must be made
Of her who often prayed,
Last century, for repose;
And the fair girl long ago
Whom I often tried to know
May be entering this rose.

So, they are not underground,
But as nerves and veins abound
In the growths of upper air,
And they feel the sun and rain,
And the energy again
That made them what they were!

John Constable, 'Cloud Study: Stormy Sunset' (*c.* 1821)

THE LAST SIGNAL

A MEMORY OF WILLIAM BARNES

11 October 1886

SILENTLY I footed by an uphill road
    That led from my abode to a spot yew-boughed;
Yellowly the sun sloped low down to westward,
    And dark was the east with cloud.

Then, amid the shadow of that livid sad east,
    Where the light was least, and a gate stood wide,
Something flashed the fire of the sun that was facing it,
    Like a brief blaze on that side.

Looking hard and harder I knew what it meant —
    The sudden shine sent from the livid east scene;
It meant the west mirrored
                by the coffin of my friend there,
    Turning to the road from his green,

To take his last journey forth — he who in his prime
    Trudged so many a time from that gate
                    athwart the land!
Thus a farewell to me he signalled on his grave-way,
    As with a wave of his hand.

THE LAST PERFORMANCE

' I AM playing my oldest tunes,' declared she,
  'All the old tunes l know –
Those I learnt ever so long ago.'
– Why she should think just then she'd play them
   Silence cloaks like snow.

When I returned from the town at nightfall
   Notes continued to pour
As when I had left two hours before:
'It's the very last time,' she said in closing;
   'From now I play no more.'

A few morns onward found her fading,
   And, as her life outflew,
I thought of her playing her tunes right through;
And I felt she had known of what was coming,
   And wondered how she knew.

LOGS ON THE HEARTH

A MEMORY OF A SISTER

THE fire advances along the log
   Of the tree we felled,
Which bloomed and bore striped apples by the peck
   Till its last hour of bearing knelled.

   The fork that first my hand would reach
      And then my foot
In climbings upward inch by inch, lies now
   Sawn, sapless, darkening with soot.

Where the bark chars is where, one year,
    It was pruned, and bled –
Then overgrew the wound. But now, at last,
    Its growings all have stagnated.

My fellow-climber rises dim
    From her chilly grave –
Just as she was, her foot near mine on the bending limb,
    Laughing, her young brown hand awave.

In Time of 'The Breaking of Nations'

(Jeremiah li: 20)

I

Only a man harrowing clods
    In a slow silent walk
With an old horse that stumbles and nods
    Half asleep as they stalk.

II

Only thin smoke without flame
    From the heaps of couch-grass;
Yet this will go onward the same
    Though Dynasties pass.

III

Yonder a maid and her wight
    Come whispering by:
War's annals will cloud into night
    Ere their story die.

THE COMING OF THE END

How it came to an end!
  The meeting afar from the crowd,
And the love-looks and laughters unpenned.
The parting when much was avowed,
    How it came to an end!

It came to an end;
Yes, the outgazing over the stream,
With the sun on each serpentine bend,
Or, later, the luring moon-gleam;
    It came to an end.

It came to an end,
The housebuilding, furnishing, planting,
As if there were ages to spend
In welcoming, feasting, and jaunting;
    It came to an end.

It came to an end,
That journey of one day a week:
('It always goes on,' said a friend,
'Just the same in bright weathers or bleak;')
    But it came to an end.

'*How* will come to an end
This orbit so smoothly begun,
Unless some convulsion attend?'
I often said. 'What will be done
    When it comes to an end?'

Well, it came to an end
Quite silently – stopped without jerk;
Better close no prevision could lend;
Working out as One planned it should work
    Ere it came to an end.

THE GARDEN SEAT

ITS former green is blue and thin,
And its once firm legs sink in and in;
Soon it will break down unaware,
Soon it will break down unaware.

At night when reddest flowers are black
Those who once sat thereon come back;
Quite a row of them sitting there,
Quite a row of them sitting there.

With them the seat does not break down,
Nor winter freeze them, nor floods drown,
For they are as light as upper air,
They are as light as upper air!

AFTERWARDS

WHEN the Present has latched its postern
    behind my tremulous stay,
 And the May month flaps its glad green leaves
      like wings,
Delicate-filmed as new-spun silk, will the neighbours say,
 'He was a man who used to notice such things'?

If it be in the dusk when, like an eyelid's soundless blink,
 The dewfall-hawk comes crossing the shades to alight
Upon the wind-warped upland thorn, a gazer may think,
 'To him this must have been a familiar sight.'

If I pass during some nocturnal blackness,
     mothy and warm,
 When the hedgehog travels furtively over the lawn,
One may say, 'He strove that such innocent creatures
     should come to no harm,
 But he could do little for them; and now he is gone.'

If, when hearing that I have been stilled at last,
     they stand at the door,
 Watching the full-starred heavens that winter sees,
Will this thought rise on those
    who will meet my face no more,
 'He was one who had an eye for such mysteries'?

And will any say when my bell of quittance
     is heard in the gloom,
 And a crossing breeze cuts a pause in its outrollings,
Till they rise again, as they were a new bell's boom,
 'He hears it not now, but used to notice such things'?

'I SOMETIMES THINK'

FOR F.E.H.

I SOMETIMES think as here I sit
   Of things I have done,
Which seemed in doing not unfit
    To face the sun:
Yet never a soul has paused a whit
    On such — not one.

There was that eager strenuous press
    To sow good seed;
There was that saving from distress
    In the nick of need;
There were those words in the wilderness:
    Who cared to heed?

Yet can this be full true, or no?
    For one did care,
And, spiriting into my house, to, fro,
    Like wind on the stair,
Cares still, heeds all, and will, even though
    I may despair.

'THE CURTAINS NOW ARE DRAWN'

SONG

I

THE curtains now are drawn,
  And the spindrift strikes the glass,
Blown up the jaggèd pass
By the surly salt sou'-west,
And the sneering glare is gone
Behind the yonder crest,
    While she sings to me:
'O the dream that thou art my Love, be it thine,
And the dream that I am thy Love, be it mine,
And death may come, but loving is divine.'

II

I stand here in the rain,
  With its smite upon her stone,
And the grasses that have grown
Over women, children, men,
And their texts that 'Life is vain;'
But I hear the notes as when
    Once she sang to me:
'O the dream that thou art my Love, be it thine,
And the dream that I am thy Love, be it mine,
And death may come, but loving is divine.'

John Atkinson Grimshaw, 'The Lovers'

WELCOME HOME

B ACK to my native place
 Bent upon returning,
Bosom all day burning
To be where my race
Well were known, 'twas keen with me
There to dwell in amity.

Folk had sought their beds,
But I hailed: to view me
Under the moon, out to me
Several pushed their heads,
And to each I told my name,
Plans, and that therefrom I came.

'Did you? ... Ah, 'tis true,'
Said they, 'back a long time,
Here had spent his young time,
Some such man as you ...
Good-night.' The casement closed again,
And I was left in the frosty lane.

'A MAN WAS DRAWING NEAR TO ME'

O N that gray night of mournful drone,
 Apart from aught to hear, to see,
I dreamt not that from shires unknown
 In gloom, alone,
 By Halworthy,
A man was drawing near to me.

I'd no concern at anything,
No sense of coming pull-heart play;
Yet, under the silent outspreading
    Of even's wing
    Where Otterham lay,
A man was riding up my way.

I thought of nobody — not of one,
But only of trifles — legends, ghosts —
Though, on the moorland dim and dun
    That travellers shun
    About these coasts,
The man had passed Tresparret Posts.

There was no light at all inland,
Only the seaward pharos-fire,
Nothing to let me understand
    That hard at hand
    By Hennett Byre
The man was getting nigh and nigher.

There was a rumble at the door,
A draught disturbed the drapery,
And but a minute passed before,
    With gaze that bore
    My destiny,
The man revealed himself to me.

Max Gate

THE STRANGE HOUSE

MAX GATE, A.D. 2000

' I HEAR the piano playing —
    Just as a ghost might play.'
'— O, but what are you saying?
    There's no piano to-day;
Their old one was sold and broken;
    Years past it went amiss.'
'— I heard it, or shouldn't have spoken:
    A strange house, this!

'I catch some undertone here,
    From someone out of sight.'
'— Impossible; we are alone here,
    And shall be through the night.'
'— The parlour-door — what stirred it?'
    '— No one: no soul's in range.'
'— But, anyhow, I heard it,
    And it seems strange!

'Seek my own room I cannot —
    A figure is on the stair!'
'— What figure? Nay, I scan not
    Any one lingering there.
A bough outside is waving,
    And that's its shade by the moon.'
'— Well, all is strange! I am craving
    Strength to leave soon.'

'— Ah, maybe you've some vision
    Of showings beyond our sphere;
Some sight, sense, intuition
    Of what once happened here?
The house is old; they've hinted
    It once held two love-thralls,
And they may have imprinted
    Their dreams on its walls?

'They were — I think 'twas told me —
    Queer in their works and ways;
The teller would often hold me
    With weird tales of those days.
Some folk can not abide here,
    But we — we do not care
Who loved, laughed, wept, or died here,
    Knew joy, or despair.'

A NIGHT IN NOVEMBER

I MARKED when the weather changed,
  And the panes began to quake,
And the winds rose up and ranged,
  That night, lying half-awake.

Dead leaves blew into my room,
  And alighted upon my bed,
And a tree declared to the gloom
  Its sorrow that they were shed.

One leaf of them touched my hand,
  And I thought that it was you
There stood as you used to stand,
  And saying at last you knew!

THE SELFSAME SONG

A BIRD sings the selfsame song,
     With never a fault in its flow,
That we listened to here those long
     Long years ago.

A pleasing marvel is how
A strain of such rapturous rote
Should have gone on thus till now
     Unchanged in a note!

— But it's not the selfsame bird.
No: perished to dust is he. ...
As also are those who heard
     That song with me.

'SHE DID NOT TURN'

SHE did not turn,
     But passed foot-faint with averted head
In her gown of green, by the bobbing fern,
Though I leaned over the gate that led
From where we waited with table spread;
     But she did not turn:
Why was she near there if love had fled?

     She did not turn,
Though the gate was whence I had often sped
In the mists of morning to meet her, and learn
Her heart, when its moving moods I read
As a book — she mine, as she sometimes said;
     But she did not turn,
And passed foot-faint with averted head.

A Two-Years' Idyll

Yes; such it was;
    Just those two seasons unsought,
Sweeping like summertide wind on our ways;
      Moving, as straws,
    Hearts quick as ours in those days;
Going like wind, too, and rated as nought
    Save as the prelude to plays
    Soon to come – larger, life-fraught:
      Yes; such it was.

     'Nought' it was called,
    Even by ourselves – that which springs
Out of the years for all flesh, first or last,
      Commonplace, scrawled
    Dully on days that go past.
Yet, all the while, it upbore us like wings
    Even in hours overcast:
    Aye, though this best thing of things,
      'Nought' it was called!

     What seems it now?
    Lost: such beginning was all;
Nothing came after: romance straight forsook
      Quickly somehow
    Life when we sped from our nook,
Primed for new scenes with designs smart and tall. ...
    – A preface without any book,
    A trumpet uplipped, but no call;
      That seems it now.

'If You Had Known'

I f you had known
　When listening with her to the far-down moan
Of the white-selvaged and empurpled sea,
And rain came on that did not hinder talk,
Or damp your flashing facile gaiety
In turning home, despite the slow wet walk
By crooked ways, and over stiles of stone;
　If you had known

　You would lay roses,
Fifty years thence, on her monument, that discloses
Its graying shape upon the luxuriant green;
Fifty years thence to an hour, by chance led there,
What might have moved you? – yea, had you foreseen
That on the tomb of the selfsame one, gone where
The dawn of every day is as the close is,
　You would lay roses!

Epitaph

I never cared for Life: Life cared for me,
　And hence I owed it some fidelity.
It now says, 'Cease; at length thou hast learnt to grind
Sufficient toll for an unwilling mind,
And I dismiss thee – not without regard
That thou didst ask no ill-advised reward,
Nor sought in me much more than thou couldst find.'

A WOMAN'S TRUST

IF he should live a thousand years
    He'd find it not again
      That scorn of him by men
Could less disturb a woman's trust
In him as a steadfast star which must
Rise scathless from the nether spheres:
If he should live a thousand years
    He'd find it not again.

She waited like a little child,
    Unchilled by damps of doubt,
      While from her eyes looked out
A confidence sublime as Spring's
When stressed by Winter's loiterings.
Thus, howsoever the wicked wiled,
She waited like a little child
    Unchilled by damps of doubt.

Through cruel years and crueller
    Thus she believed in him
      And his aurore, so dim;
That, after fenweeds, flowers would blow;
And above all things did she show
Her faith in his good faith with her;
Through cruel years and crueller
    Thus she believed in him!

LAST WEEK IN OCTOBER

THE trees are undressing, and fling in many places –
  On the gray road, the roof, the window-sill –
Their radiant robes and ribbons and yellow laces;
A leaf each second so is flung at will,
Here, there, another and another, still and still.

A spider's web has caught one while downcoming,
  That stays there dangling when the rest pass on;
Like a suspended criminal hangs he, mumming
  In golden garb, while one yet green, high yon,
Trembles, as fearing such a fate for himself anon.

TEN YEARS SINCE

'TIS ten years since
  I saw her on the stairs,
  Heard her in house-affairs,
  And listened to her cares;
And the trees are ten feet taller,
And the sunny spaces smaller
Whose bloomage would enthrall her;
And the piano wires are rustier,
The smell of bindings mustier,
And lofts and lumber dustier
  Than when, with casual look
  And ear, light note I took
  Of what shut like a book
    Those ten years since!

WHEN DEAD

TO —

I T will be much better when
I am under the bough;
I shall be more myself, Dear, then,
Than I am now.

No sign of querulousness
To wear you out
Shall I show there: strivings and stress
Be quite without.

This fleeting life-brief blight
Will have gone past
When I resume my old and right
Place in the Vast.

And when you come to me
To show you true,
Doubt not I shall infallibly
Be waiting you.

NIGHT-TIME IN MID-FALL

I T is a storm-strid night, winds footing swift
Through the blind profound;
I know the happenings from their sound;
Leaves totter down still green, and spin and drift;
The tree-trunks rock to their roots,

which wrench and lift
The loam where they run onward underground.

The streams are muddy and swollen; eels migrate
    To a new abode;
    Even cross, 'tis said, the turnpike-road;
(Men's feet have felt their crawl, home-coming late):
The westward fronts of towers are saturate,
Church-timbers crack, and witches ride abroad.

NOBODY COMES

TREE-LEAVES labour up and down,
    And through them the fainting light
    Succumbs to the crawl of night.
Outside in the road the telegraph wire
    To the town from the darkening land
Intones to travellers like a spectral lyre
    Swept by a spectral hand.

A car comes up, with lamps full-glare,
    That flash upon a tree:
    It has nothing to do with me,
And whangs along in a world of its own,
    Leaving a blacker air;
And mute by the gate I stand again alone,
    And nobody pulls up there.

No Buyers

A STREET SCENE

A LOAD of brushes and baskets
             and cradles and chairs
   Labours along the street in the rain:
With it a man, a woman, a pony with whiteybrown hairs.
   The man foots in front of the horse
                   with a shambling sway
     At a slower tread than a funeral train,
   While to a dirge-like tune he chants his wares,
Swinging a Turk's-head brush (in a drum-major's way
     When the bandsmen march and play).

A yard from the back of the man
            is the whiteybrown pony's nose:
He mirrors his master in every item of pace and pose:
     He stops when the man stops, without being told,
   And seems to be eased by a pause; too plainly he's old,
      Indeed, not strength enough shows
     To steer the disjointed waggon straight,
   Which wriggles left and right in a rambling line,
   Deflected thus by its own warp and weight,
   And pushing the pony with it in each incline.

     The woman walks on the pavement verge,
       Parallel to the man:
   She wears an apron white and wide in span,
And carries a like Turk's-head, but more in nursing wise:
     Now and then she joins in his dirge,
     But as if her thoughts were on distant things.
     The rain clams her apron till it clings. —
   So, step by step, they move with their merchandise,
     And nobody buys.

'NOTHING MATTERS MUCH'

B.F.L.

'NOTHING matters much,' he said
    Of something just befallen unduly:
He, then active, but now dead,
    Truly, truly!

He knew the letter of the law
As voiced by those of wig and gown,
Whose slightest syllogistic flaw
    He hammered down.

And often would he shape in word
That nothing needed much lamenting;
And she who sat there smiled and heard,
    Sadly assenting.

Facing the North Sea now he lies,
Toward the red altar of the East,
The Flamborough roar his psalmodies,
    The wind his priest.

And while I think of his bleak bed,
Of Time that builds, of Time that shatters,
Lost to all thought is he, who said
    'Nothing much matters.'

'Why Do I?'

Why do I go on doing these things?
      Why not cease?
Is it that you are yet in this world of welterings
      And unease,
And that, while so, mechanic repetitions please?

   When shall I leave off doing these things? —
      When I hear
You have dropped your dusty cloak
                              and taken your wondrous wings
      To another sphere,
Where no pain is: Then shall I hush this dinning gear.

THOUGHTS AT MIDNIGHT

MANKIND, you dismay me
When shadows waylay me! —
Not by your splendours
Do you affray me,
Not as pretenders
To demonic keenness,
Not by your meanness,
Nor your ill-teachings,
Nor your false preachings,
Nor your banalities
And immoralities,
Nor by your daring
Nor sinister bearing;
But by your madnesses
Capping cool badnesses,
Acting like puppets
Under Time's buffets;
In superstitions
And ambitions
Moved by no wisdom,
Far-sight, or system,
Led by sheer senselessness
And presciencelessness
Into unreason
And hideous self-treason. ...
God, look he on you,
Have mercy upon you!

THE LOVE-LETTERS

IN MEMORIAM H.R.

I MET him quite by accident
In a bye-path that he'd frequent.
And, as he neared, the sunset glow
Warmed up the smile of pleasantry
Upon his too thin face, while he
Held a square packet up to me,
    Of what, I did not know.

'Well,' said he then; 'they are my old letters.
Perhaps she — rather felt them fetters. ...
You see, I am in a slow decline,
And she's broken off with me. Quite right
To send them back, and true foresight;
I'd got too fond of her! Tonight
    I burn them — stuff of mine!'

He laughed in the sun — an ache in his laughter —
And went. I heard of his death soon after.

THE MOUND

For a moment pause: —
     Just here it was;
And through the thin thorn hedge,
                    by the rays of the moon,
I can see the tree in the field, and beside it the mound —
Now sheeted with snow — whereon we sat that June
     When it was green and round,
And she crazed my mind by what she coolly told —
     The history of her undoing,
(As I saw it), but she called 'comradeship,'
     That bred in her no rueing:
     And saying she'd not be bound
For life to one man, young, ripe-yeared, or old,
Left me — an innocent simpleton to her viewing;
For, though my accompt of years outscored her own,
     Hers had more hotly flown. ...
We never met again by this green mound,
To press as once so often lip on lip,
     And palter, and pause: —
     Yes; here it was!

EVENING SHADOWS

The shadows of my chimneys stretch afar
     Across the plot, and on to the privet bower,
And even the shadows of their smokings show,
And nothing says just now that where they are
They will in future stretch at this same hour,
Though in my earthen cyst I shall not know.

And at this time the neighbouring Pagan mound,
Whose myths the Gospel news now supersede,
Upon the greensward also throws its shade,
And nothing says such shade will spread around
Even as to-day when men will no more heed
The Gospel news than when the mound was made.

THROWING A TREE

NEW FOREST

THE two executioners stalk along over the knolls,
　Bearing two axes with heavy heads
　　　　　　　　　　　shining and wide,
And a long limp two-handled saw
　　　　　　　　toothed for cutting great boles,
And so they approach the proud tree
　　　　　　　that bears the death-mark on its side.

Jackets doffed they swing axes
　　　　　　　　　and chop away just above ground,
And the chips fly about
　　　　　　　and lie white on the moss and fallen leaves;
Till a broad deep gash in the bark
　　　　　　　　　is hewn all the way round,
And one of them tries to hook upward a rope,
　　　　　　　　　which at last he achieves.

The saw then begins,
                    till the top of the tall giant shivers:
The shivers are seen
                    to grow greater each cut than before:
They edge out the saw, tug the rope;
                    but the tree only quivers,
And kneeling and sawing again,
                    they step back to try pulling once more.

Then, lastly, the living mast sways, further sways:
                    with a shout
Job and Ike rush aside.
                    Reached the end of its long staying powers
The tree crashes downward:
                    it shakes all its neighbours throughout,
And two hundred years' steady growth
                    has been ended in less than two hours.

The Lodging-House Fuchsias

Mrs Masters's fuchsias hung
Higher and broader, and brightly swung,
    Bell-like, more and more
Over the narrow garden-path,
Giving the passer a sprinkle-bath
    In the morning.

She put up with their pushful ways,
And made us tenderly lift their sprays,
    Going to her door:
But when her funeral had to pass
They cut back all the flowery mass
    In the morning.

Asker Durand, 'The Beeches' (1845)

LYING AWAKE

You, Morningtide Star, now are steady-eyed,
                              over the east,
  I know it as if I saw you;
You, Beeches, engrave on the sky your thin twigs,
                              even the least;
  Had I paper and pencil I'd draw you.

You, Meadow, are white
                    with your counterpane cover of dew,
  I see it as if I were there;
You, Churchyard, are lightening faint
                         from the shade of the yew,
  The names creeping out everywhere.

SUSPENSE

A CLAMMINESS hangs over all like a clout,
  The fields are a water-colour washed out,
The sky at its rim leaves a chink of light,
Like the lid of a pot that will not close tight.

She is away by the groaning sea,
Strained at the heart, and waiting for me:
Between us our foe from a hid retreat
Is watching, to wither us if we meet. ...

But it matters little, however we fare —
Whether we meet, or I get not there;
The sky will look the same thereupon,
And the wind and the sea go groaning on.

CHRISTMAS: 1924

' PEACE upon earth!' was said. We sing it,
       And pay a million priests to bring it.
After two thousand years of mass
We've got as far as poison-gas.

'WE ARE GETTING TO THE END'

.WE are getting to the end of visioning
      The impossible within this universe,
Such as that better whiles may follow worse,
And that our race may mend by reasoning.

We know that even as larks in cages sing
Unthoughtful of deliverance from the curse
That holds them lifelong in a latticed hearse,
We ply spasmodically our pleasuring.

And that when nations set them to lay waste
Their neighbours' heritage by foot and horse,
And hack their pleasant plains in festering seams,
They may again, – not warely, or from taste,
But tickled mad by some demonic force. –
Yes. We are getting to the end of dreams!

HE RESOLVES TO SAY NO MORE

O MY soul, keep the rest unknown!
It is too like a sound of moan
   When the charnel-eyed
   Pale Horse has nighed:
Yea, none shall gather what I hide!

Why load men's minds with more to bear
That bear already ails to spare?
   From now alway
   Till my last day
What I discern I will not say.

Let Time roll backward if it will;
(Magians who drive the midnight quill
   With brain aglow
   Can see it so,)
What I have learnt no man shall know.

And if my vision range beyond
The blinkered sight of souls in bond,
   — By truth made free —
   I'll let all be,
And show to no man what I see.

Index of First Lines

A bird sings the selfsame song............................89

A clamminess hangs over all like a clout.............105

A load of brushes and baskets and cradles and........96

As some bland soul, to whom a debtor says..........47

Back to my native place..................................84

Breathe not, hid Heart: cease silently.................34

Christmas Eve, and twelve of the clock...............72

Close up the casement, draw the blind................45

Con the dead page as 'twere live love: press on!....35

Everybody else, then, going.............................66

For a moment pause.....................................101

Had he and I but met....................................51

He does not think that I haunt here nightly..........61

Here by the moorway you returned.....................64

Here is the ancient floor................................39

How it came to an end!..................................78

'I am playing my oldest tunes,' declared she.........76

I am the family face......................................70

I determined to find out whose it was.................70

I have risen again..63

I hear the piano playing.................................87

I leant upon a coppice gate.............................38

I longed to love a full-boughed beech.................23

I look into my glass......................................27

I marked when the weather changed...................88

I met him quite by accident............................100

I never cared for Life: Life cared for me..............91

I saw a dead man's finer part..........................37

I say, 'I'll seek her side................................46

I sometimes think as here I sit.........................81

If but some vengeful god would call to me..........17

If he should live a thousand years.....................92

If you had known 91
In five-score summers! All new eyes.................... 46
It is a storm-strid night, winds footing swift.......... 94
It will be much better when 94
Its former green is blue and thin........................ 79
Mankind, you dismay me 99
Mrs Masters's fuchsias hung 103
My spirit will not haunt the mound.................... 54
Not a line of her writing have I 26
'Nothing matters much,' he said........................ 97
O life with the sad seared face 31
O my soul, keep the rest unknown! 107
On afternoons of drowsy calm........................... 68
On that gray night of mournful drone 84
Only a man harrowing clods 77
'Peace upon earth!' was said. We sing it............ 106
Perhaps, long hence, when I have passed away....... 19
'Poor wanderer,' said the leaden sky 32
Portion of this yew.. 73
She did not turn 89
She sits in the tawny vapour 29
Silently I footed by an uphill road 75
Sinking down by the gate I discern the thin moon ... 53
Somewhere afield here something lies................. 30
That mirror... 67
That night your great guns, unawares 52
The curtains now are drawn............................. 82
The fire advances along the log 76
The grey gaunt days dividing us in twain.............. 50
The Roman Road runs straight and bare 50
The shadows of my chimneys stretch afar 101
The singers are gone from the Cornmarket-place ... 48
The trees are undressing, and fling in many places .. 93
The two executioners stalk along over the knolls.. 102

The two were silent in a sunless church 18
The wind blew words along the skies 72
There are some heights in Wessex, shaped as if by .. 54
There floated the sounds of church-chiming 69
There have been times when I well might have 42
They bear him to his resting-place 17
They throw in Drummer Hodge, to rest 28
Though I waste watches framing words to fetter 18
'Tis ten years since 93
Tree-leaves labour up and down 95
Upon a noon I pilgrimed through 21
Upon a poet's page I wrote 20
We are getting to the end of visioning 106
We sat at the window looking out 68
We stood by a pond that winter day 20
When I walked roseless tracks and wide 71
When the clouds' swoln bosoms echo back the 41
When the Present has latched its postern behind 80
Whenever I plunge my arm, like this 58
Why did you give no hint that night 60
Why do I go on doing these things? 98
William Dewy, Tranter Reuben, Farmer Ledlow ... 24
Wintertime nighs 40
Woman much missed, how you call to me, call to .. 65
Yes; such it was 90
You did not come 36
You, Morningtide Star, now are steady-eyed 105